COUNTRY LIVING

Seasons at
Seven Gates Farm

COUNTRY LIVING

Seasons at Seven Gates Farm

Decorating in the Country Tradition

Photographs by

KEITH SCOTT MORTON

Text by

MARY SEEHAFER SEARS

HEARST BOOKS
A Division of Sterling Publishing Co., Inc.
New York

COPYRIGHT © 1996 BY HEARST COMMUNICATIONS, INC.

PRODUCED BY SMALLWOOD & STEWART, INC., NEW YORK CITY
EDITOR • RACHEL CARLEY
ART DIRECTOR • SUSI OBERHELMAN
DESIGNER • PAT TAN
ILLUSTRATOR • WENDY FROST

Photographs on pages 178–181 by Dean Johnson

Library of Congress Cataloging-in-Publication Data
Available upon request.

10 9 8 7 6 5 4 3 2 1

First Paperback Edition 2003
Published by Hearst Books
A Division of Sterling Publishing Co., Inc.
387 Park Avenue South, New York, NY 10016

Country Living and Hearst Books are trademarks owned by
Hearst Magazines Property, Inc., in USA,
and Hearst Communications, Inc., in Canada.

www.countryliving.com

Distributed in Canada by Sterling Publishing
c/o Canadian Manda Group, One Atlantic Avenue, Suite 105
Toronto, Ontario, Canada M6K 3E7
Distributed in Australia by Capricorn Link (Australia) Pty. Ltd.
P.O. Box 704, Windsor, NSW 2756 Australia

Printed in China

ISBN 1-58816-264-8

c   o   n   t

AUTUMN 132

WINTER 174

e   n   t   s

fore

word

When one has spent as many years as I have meeting, writing about and photographing creative people, one develops a sixth sense about who is competent, who has real talent, and who has reached through the boundaries into the extraordinary. James Cramer is one of those who has gone beyond the boundaries. From the time his home was first shown in *Country Living*, it was clear that Jimmie's aesthetic, his color sense and his feel for gathering and blending antiques with flora was uniquely inspiring. With his partner Dean Johnson, a craftsman of equally extraordinary talents, Jimmie creates a year round revolving fantasy in his home and garden. We are fortunate at *Country Living* to have discovered Jimmie and proudly list him as our Editor-at-Large. His boundless energy, unbridled enthusiasm and spirited approach to all that he creates serve to make Jimmie truly "one of a kind." This book will bring you into the world of Jimmie and Dean, Seven Gates Farm. Enjoy your stay!

Rachel Newman
Editor Emerita, *Country Living*

INTROD

Welcome to Seven Gates Farm. Tucked in a quiet corner of northwestern Maryland, this charming 19th-century home-

stead (pictured in 1886, left) now serves as workplace, studio, and home to James Cramer and Dean Johnson. The two men, who are both accomplished artists, craftsmen, and gardeners, purchased the farm in 1984 and have been tending to its well-being ever since. In the process, Seven Gates has become the inspiration for countless original decorating ideas, natural handcrafts, and homespun country holidays throughout the year. ❦ The story

U C T I O N

of Seven Gates begins more than 150 years ago, when a two-story log farmhouse was built in the rural hamlet of Centerville, now known as Keedysville. Believed to date to about 1830, the house was owned by the Wyand family, who lovingly passed it from generation to generation. Typical of its time and place, the two-story house had a pair of front parlors, a rear kitchen, and two more rooms upstairs. A log smokehouse stood to the west; nearby was the wood-frame summer kitchen, which was also used as a washhouse (shown generations later in a 1956 Wyand family photo, right). A walnut tree towered behind

the side yard, apple trees bloomed in the rear orchard, and autumn crocuses were planted by the front porch. 🖋 In time, the Wyands and their descendants made improvements. The log walls of the farmhouse were eventually faced with more fashionable brick, as was the custom in the area. By the 1880s a picket fence fronted the street side of the property and the roof had been raised over the kitchen ell to make another upstairs room. 🖋 Almost all of the farm's 250 acres were sold off bit by bit, but the house ~ with the original mantels, doors, and locks in place ~ remained in the Wyand family until James and Dean purchased it along with a one-acre parcel of land. Although the farm was in disrepair, they were taken with the old outbuildings and the solid house with its wide Victorian porch. They were also captivated by the history of the place: During the Civil War, the Wyand barn (now owned by a neighbor) had served as a hospital. As luck would have it, the family living across the street turned out to be relatives of the Wyands, with lots of photographs and stories to share about the old house. James and Dean respected the farm's past as they renovated the buildings and planted the gardens, and now their lives are entwined with its history, too. ❧ The men moved in during the spring, and though the house needed attention, they planted the gardens first. Their instincts seemed indulgent at the time, but proved to be wise. "Gardens take time," they reflect. "We wish we could have planted even sooner, so everything would be further along."  While they collaborate on many projects, some of the tasks at hand fall naturally to the talents of each. James (with Elijah, their trusted Yorkie, right) is the self-appointed caretaker of the gardens and  farmhouse. In warm weather he spends his time in the greenhouse and yard; during cold months he settles into his second-story studio in the farmhouse (above). There he makes seasonal decorations, including his signature wooden-winged Christmas angels, and paints Dean's miniature greenhouses, known as cloches.

Dean (right) is a woodworker; the rustic

fences, arbors, trellises, scarecrows, bird-

houses, and wooden cloches everywhere

evident at Seven Gates Farm are invariably crafted by his

talented hands. His workshop ("mostly tools and sawdust," he

says) occupies the former carriage house (below left). ✒ Like

the country artists of days long past, the two men make a living

selling their handwork and participate in a

few select juried shows in New England

and the mid-Atlantic states each year.

They are both knowledgeable collectors

and share an interest in antique textiles and miniature log houses. ❧ James was born and raised in central Maryland and Dean is from eastern Tennessee; traditions like their New Year's Day brunch of good-luck foods blend customs, many recalled from childhood, from both areas. They approach life at the farm with straightforward simplicity and good common sense. Firm believers in recycling, the men haunt flea markets and antiques shops and have made an art of improvisation; indeed, little at Seven Gates is ever bought new. Flowers are transplanted, balled-root Christmas trees are given homes outdoors when the holidays end, and almost every object finds a new use when its first life is over. The men emphasize that even the most simple belongings can create atmosphere and a sense of place, as long as they have personal meaning. At the heart of any well-loved home, they say, is the spirit of change. Constantly rearranging favorite belongings as the seasons pass is part of the pleasure of making a house your own. ❧ Nothing illustrates that kind of natural evolution more clearly than a year in the life of Seven Gates Farm. We at *Country Living* are especially pleased to invite you inside the front gate to share an extended visit. Wherever you live, we hope that a journey through the seasons with James Cramer and Dean Johnson will inspire you as much as it has us. ❧

Mary Seehafer Sears

S   P   R

Muddy boots and gardening gloves clutter the  back porch, shears are shined and sharpened in the shed, and it's clear a new season has arrived at Seven Gates Farm. In April, the fear that winter might never end is assuaged when the first snowdrops and lilies-of-the-valley, talismans of gardeners who lived here long ago, finally poke up around the front porch. 🐟 A few weeks after Easter,  the apple orchard erupts in a fabulous show of white. The blossoming trees are skirted by a carpet of pale Mount Hood daffodils, spaced naturally according to an old-time custom passed on by a friend (bulbs are tossed, then planted wherever they happen to land).

I   N   G

❧ Around the perimeter of the farm, other spring flowers, including hyacinths, crocuses, tulips, and jonquils, put on a showy display, hailing the start of the season's outdoor projects. There are bird feeders to scrub, raking to be done, and seedlings to move from green-  house to gardens. ❧ Once the beds are readied, it's time to air the farmhouse; doors and windows are thrown open to usher in fresh breezes and clear away winter cobwebs. James and Dean set aside one bright Saturday to polish the floors and wash

 the windows inside and out, in sure belief that sparkling surfaces ~ and big bouquets of spring flowers ~ are all it takes to make a house shine. ❧

the green

"When seedlings start to sprout, we know that spring can't be far away."

house

A richly sculptural Italianate-style door pediment discovered at an antiques shop and a salvaged cast-iron gate fronting a storage bin for flowerpots bring great character to the prefabricated greenhouse (opposite). It took just two days to put together the 8½-by-20-foot structure, made of teleflex mylar stretched over an aluminum frame. "The key is to have everything level and square when you start and it will finish up just right," says Dean, who spent another day building the pine potting benches inside (overleaf).

Long before spring officially arrives in this corner of western Maryland, it blossoms in the backyard greenhouse. Here, James nurtures his topiary plants through the winter and, as early as the end of February, starts annuals for the gardens from seeds.

Of course, this is no ordinary greenhouse. Although it was built from a mail-order kit, quirky old architectural elements and other customizing touches transformed what might have been a featureless outbuilding into an inviting year-round haven for both plants and gardeners. Indeed, the two men turned the same critical eye to decorating the space as they would to any room inside their house. Among the more unusual embellishments are salvaged columns (ideal for plant pedestals), an antique fanlight recycled as a wall sculpture, a 19th-century door pediment, and James's working collection of antique garden implements, which includes brass sprinkler heads, watering cans, and terra-cotta flowerpots from England and Europe. Any of the smaller items might be put to their rightful use ~ or borrowed for artful and ever-changing still lifes to catch the eye.

Yet, while there is admittedly much to please the senses, this

*In this greenhouse, there is much
more to delight the eye than plants.
A folk art birdhouse (above left)
is a replica of the capitol building in
Richmond, Virginia. Dean's own
design for a miniature greenhouse,
which he calls a cloche (above right),
features tiny acrylic windows.*

greenhouse also works hard. Generously proportioned potting
benches ~ slatted so air can circulate and prevent warping ~ run the
length of both side walls, providing plenty of storage room for pots
and garden flats. A layer of brown river pebbles spread over a base
of crushed stone, laid directly on a dirt base, helps keep moisture
in and sounds a satisfying crunch underfoot. Adjustable windows,
finished with ribbed surfaces to filter a gentle light, make it easy
to regulate the temperature.

This hospitable setting is ideal for starting trays of tomato and
cabbage seedlings, as well as geraniums, impatiens, marigolds, and
daisies. James also starts many plants from cuttings, propagating

Telltale signs of spring: Upended French melon pots, a bundle of raffia for tying topiaries, and an English terra-cotta seed tray form a tableau on James's worktable (top). Irises sprout from antique bulb pots in the filtered light under the slatted potting benches (left); seed pots, broken and whole, become an unexpected still life in a clay pot amid a mix of mosses and germander (above).

A hollow zinc porch column supports a pot of heart-shaped ivy (right); the salvaged fanlight is mounted with hooks and eyes. James created a charming surprise by training ivy around pine-needle nests with florist's pins (below left). Propped up on a bit of broken flowerpot ~ so they won't decay when the ivy is watered ~ the nests hold dried quails' eggs purchased from Amish farmers. A pair of painted columns (below right) was found at an Ohio antiques show.

myrtle, germander, begonias, rosemary, thyme, and even antique roses in small protective boxes known as cloches. Designed and built by Dean, these miniature greenhouses are placed over young potted plants to generate warmth from the sun. Bottomless versions can also be moved outdoors to protect young starts in the garden, permitting the men to put some plants out well before May 15, the traditional planting date in this area of Maryland.

The greenhouse is also a perfect environment for the topiaries. These thrive here all winter and James spends many a morning trimming them into shape. He waters the topiaries early in the day, and again in the afternoon if the sun is out and they seem dry. Each

Irish moss sprouting from the soil made an impromptu ruffle for a potted myrtle (above left). Double and triple topiaries (above right) take four to six years to reach this size. In winter, the plants can be kept in any sunny window. In summer, they are gradually acclimated to the outdoors, first in a shady spot for a few days, then in full sun.

Dried grapevines wrapped around the side-gate arbor (above) provide a natural foothold for white Floribunda roses, which will bloom in summer. A hearthstone from an old log cabin dominates the dooryard (opposite); the river stones were purchased at a quarry. Planting arbor vitae (overleaf) proved an ingenious way to fill in the corner gaps of the recycled fence. As they fill out, these trees will add structure and color to the yard, especially important in winter when the rest of the garden is bare.

year, the manicured plants are transplanted into slightly larger pots. Any that are more than a year old move outdoors for the summer.

Just outside the greenhouse, a picket fence, gates, and arbor help define its space within the larger yard. The fence arrived one day in 13 separate sections on the back of the truck of a local antiques dealer who was bringing it home to his shop from New England. "I bought it on the spot," says James. The fence, which had its original finials but no posts, was clearly going to run short of the desired size. But at Seven Gates Farm, no problem goes without a solution: Dean built new posts and James "stretched" the enclosure by planting an evergreen at each corner.

myrtle topiary

A. Fill a pot with soil and transplant the myrtle. Clip all secondary branches, leaving 10 to 15 leaves at the stem top. Insert a stake in the soil, being careful not to disturb the plant's roots. Tie the stem to the stake at 2-inch intervals with raffia.

B. Place the pot in sunny window. As the plant grows, continue trimming the stem of all side growth, but do not cut top growth. The raffia knots will decay and pop as the stem grows; replace as needed. Rotate the pot daily to prevent the stem from leaning.

C. When the plant has grown 2 inches above the stake, pinch back the growing tip. When the branches have thickened (this will take several months), trim the top growth into a smooth globe shape. Groom the ball periodically as it fills out.

From fragile beginning to full maturation, a topiary ~ any plant that has been coaxed and clipped into a decorative shape ~ is a labor of love. The myrtles shown here are slow to take form (it takes a year to grow a golf-ball-size globe) but will live indefinitely with proper care. Watering daily at the same time prevents leaves from dropping; to avoid brown spots, water should flow from the bottom of the pot, which keeps air pockets from forming in the soil. Monthly feeding with fertilizer designed for shrubs (30-10-10) is recommended. Young myrtle plants are available in spring at garden centers; sweet bay and rosemary will give equally good results. Choose a healthy seedling with a straight primary stem about 4 inches tall. Materials and equipment: myrtle plants; pots; potting soil; scissors; plant stakes (in 12-inch, 18-inch, and 24-inch sizes); raffia.

in the

gardens

Constantly tended and rearranged, the gardens at Seven Gates are much like a series of rooms unfolding around the yard. Shrubs and trees delineate the basic structure of the various planted areas, but within this framework each plot displays its own distinct mood and color scheme. On the south side of the house is an herb garden filled with annuals and perennials, where a path leads to the washhouse. In the rear, tucked between the washhouse and the smokehouse, is a secluded stone-paved topiary garden; opposite this, against the back of the house, a grape arbor shades a smaller terrace. A vegetable garden sprawls just in front of the greenhouse in the northwest corner of the property, and dominating the north yard is the most formal of the garden plots: a symmetrically designed white perennial garden.

Each April, the men prepare the beds by clearing them of any plants that did not make it through the winter, turning the soil and replenishing it with a compost of leaf mulch; peat moss is also scattered beneath boxwoods and trees. Then it's time to bring out the flowers. In the years that James and Dean have lived on the farm,

A brilliant flock of Oriental poppies is relegated to a field just south of the herb-garden fence where these unruly perennials can spread at will (opposite). Blooming in April, spiky purple ajuga, Salome daffodils, narcissus, and red tulips brighten the yard near the washhouse (overleaf). While the gardens feature new plants, stalwart figures like the centuries-old walnut tree towering behind the birdhouse are an important part of the landscape and endow it with a sense of history.

Planted amid chives, elegant
William and Mary tulips put on
a show of colors in late April (above).
These variegated bulbs first
flower yellow with a blush of pink,
then turn creamy white after
their pointed petals open fully. In
May, the chives burst into
delicate purple blossoms (right).

their perennial gardens have matured and a few brilliant annuals are all that is needed to fill in. James tucks impatiens, started in the greenhouse, into shady spots to add a spark of color here and there. Potted annuals also play a role. Fresh white wax begonias go into the urns flanking the white-garden arbor; although James once considered them ordinary, these plants have won his favor with their heartiness and constant blooms. White geraniums and ivy that have wintered in the greenhouse are transplanted to vintage sap buckets to decorate outdoor tables. And on the front porch, visible from the road, cheerful pansies make a yearly appearance in oak-splint egg baskets protected with plastic liners.

Planting herbs around the well in the herb garden is another rite of spring. Creeping thyme is one of the first perennials to come back on its own; James adds rosemary and more thyme grown from cuttings, along with lavender and chives started from seed. Basil and dill seeds are sown directly in the soil. Bronze fennel, lemon balm, marjoram, and savory round out the fragrant mix.

For extra interest, James and Dean make a point of adding elements besides plants to their gardens. White-painted bee skeps (above left) sit in a cedar-shingled shelter modeled after one at the Museum of Appalachia in Norris, Tennessee. Three years old, the fluffy snowball bushes flanking the skeps bloom in May. A log-cabin birdhouse crafted by Dean (above right) is a tall focal point. Planted in small clumps throughout the garden, the Salome daffodils are an encouraging sign of spring.

Sweet woodruff, a flowering
groundcover, returns year
after year to provide a carpet of
white under the grape arbor.
Ivy and geraniums in a painted
sap bucket salute the coming
of spring (above), while a concrete
bowl holds white violas and a
pine-needle nest circled with ivy
(right). Dean found the fan-
shaped trellis (opposite) at a local
auction and had to walk it
home because it was too large
to fit in his car.

using a cold frame

Best set against a south-facing wall for optimum sun, a cold frame ~ a bottomless box fitted with glass panes ~ helps gardeners get a head start on spring, protecting new plants when the weather is unreliable. A simple base can be made of wood two-by-fours or concrete blocks. Hinged at the tops, old windows are good insulators, easily propped open on warm days to prevent overheating. James covers the glass with a blanket when the temperature threatens to plunge; mounding hay around the outside will also provide extra insulation.

It is possible to supply a cold frame with potting soil and sow seeds directly, or use it as a way station for leggy seedlings started in the house or greenhouse. Seedlings can remain in their own flats, or be transplanted right into the soil for two or three weeks so they can harden off before moving into the garden. A cold frame also works well for forcing bulbs like hyacinths and tulips. Pansies will often survive the winter in this hospitable environment and barring a prolonged freeze, lettuce can be harvested throughout the year as well.

In early spring, James sets up a twig support for decorative runner beans in the vegetable garden (left) by poking crossed poles into the soil tent fashion and running horizontal connectors over the forked joints, which can be tied with raffia. Squash plants make their early debut, started from seed and protected by glass bell jars; James uses antiques as well as reproductions, available at garden shops. Tulips bloom by a birdbath (above); the "pedestal" is an upended log.

the outdoor

table

Arranging the yard is an enduring rite of spring, when outdoor furniture comes out of winter storage in the smokehouse and everything gets a fresh coat of paint ~ either sage green or a muted "whitewash" made by thinning latex paint with water. Topiaries, clay pots brimming with spring annuals, and decorations culled from James's collection of vintage garden tools make natural choices for outdoor table settings that capture the lighthearted spirit of the new season. "Almost anything will work," declares James. "Throw a beautiful shawl over the table, arrange a few flowerpots on it ~ even empty ones ~ and bring out some candles and hurricane lamps."

Placement is equally casual. There are no rules: James is apt to set a table and chairs right in the middle of the yard ~ any spot that has shade and a view qualifies. Constantly moving and replacing furniture is a natural part of the process. One favorite spot is the smokehouse terrace. On spring evenings, the two men are often found here watching the sun sink slowly behind the apple trees. "We used to work all the time," James reflects, "but now we know better and we have slowed down to appreciate what we have."

One of several garden tables that are moved at will around the yard is surrounded by a family of potted topiaries; it took eight years for the largest, behind the chair to the left, to reach this size. Younger, smaller plants become impromptu centerpieces for the table. A wine bottle is wrapped in a checked linen dish towel, with a nosegay of garden flowers tucked in the knot.

*An outdoor table designed by Dean
features a plate-glass top resting
on "arbor" cross beams and a picket-
fence base that encloses potted
daisies and geraniums (opposite).
An old bed ticking serves as a table
cloth while vintage garden tools
and a straw hat overflowing
with strawberries make amusing
table decorations (above left).
Flowerpot pockets on garden pillows
hold real seed packets, talismans
of the season (above right). A
thermos lid becomes a handy vase
for a bunch of mint (left).*

49

flowerpots

Many gardeners favor the attractive aged look of old terra-cotta pots, naturally seasoned with a layer of moss and the powdery white salts that seep through the clay from soil and fertilizers. James's own collection of garden containers includes vintage French, English, and Flemish pots, which turn up by the thousands when old commercial and estate greenhouses are torn down. "Europeans never used the plastic pots we have here; even today they prefer terra-cotta," says James. That is why so many are available, including his favorite English seed pots, barely an inch across.

Most of James's pots have been picked up by friends traveling abroad, but the European containers are turning up increasingly in American garden shops as well. Vintage clay pots of all types can also be found at antiques shows, flea markets, and estate sales.

To show off the different shapes and colors, James stacks pots in graduated sizes or piles them in baskets or wheelbarrows. Mossy pots are best set side by side to avoid disturbing the finish. (To force moss, wet a clay pot with beer and then fill it with soil or a plant. Place in a shady spot and keep moist. Soft growth should start to appear in about a month.)

Clay pots should be brought indoors before the first freeze to prevent cracking. Other than that, they need no special care. "They age themselves naturally," says James.

the upstairs

studio

A calm oasis in springtime, the upstairs studio in the farmhouse is James's workshop, where ideas are born and decorating projects begun. Tucked into a rear ell above the kitchen, this is the sunniest room in the house, with windows on all three sides overlooking the south and north gardens as well as the topiary garden in the back. The exposed log wall was the exterior of the house before the roof of the kitchen ell beneath the studio was raised many years ago; James's brother painted the floor with a checkerboard pattern of taupe and cream to complement the rustic surface.

During the warm months, James spends most of his creative hours in the gardens and greenhouse. Cleared of its clutter, the studio becomes a quiet garden room, embellished with topiaries, piles of terra-cotta pots, and the sculptural antique garden tools that he constantly rearranges into new displays both indoors and out. Come autumn, the studio will become a busy, cluttered workshop as James stitches, glues, and cuts, crafting garden accessories and decorations for the Christmas holidays. But for now, the studio is tidy and cool, a serene retreat at the top of the stairs.

In the spring, plants and tools are gathered in the studio, which becomes a quiet garden room. A tabletop greenhouse made in the 1930s rests on an 1860s harvest table from the Shenandoah Valley; next to it, a globe of grapevines cages a myrtle topiary. Vintage garden sprinklers line up on a bench under the window, while glass garden bells cluster below it. On the wall, twig frames made by Dean set off floral prints saved from a tattered gardening book.

In a zinc-lined dry sink, a miniature greenhouse propped open with a tiny shovel holds seed pots and blooming thyme (right). Plucked from the garden, sweet-pea tendrils twine around the empty picture frame. Brass hose nozzles are artfully arranged on the window sash; more of James's tool collection, including a 19th-century corn planter, is shown off on the wall (below). A graduated plant stand makes an ideal showcase for potted topiaries (opposite).

miniature garden

A. Line the box with a plastic bag folded to fit; make sure the bottom and sides are covered to prevent water and soil from seeping out. Place potting soil in the box with a trowel, leveling off at about 1 inch below the rim.

B. Arrange the aquarium pebbles on top of the soil to make a pattern of miniature pathways leading from each end of the box to a small circle in center. (Or try a variation on this pattern.)

C. Plant myrtle at 1-inch intervals along the two long sides of the box and around the outer rim of the pebble circle. As the myrtle grows, clip it to shape a minihedge. Plant the rest of the soil with thyme. Place a miniature pottery urn or other ornament in the center.

This little landscape-in-a-box is a small-scale version of a formal garden. It makes a delightful portable centerpiece that can be used by day on a patio or porch table, then brought indoors for a dinner party. The minigarden here is planted with myrtle and creeping thyme, but any low-growing groundcover will work. James recommends trying different landscape designs or adding a bent-wire trellis trained with ivy (above). The box should be watered regularly in the same manner as a house plant. Materials and equipment: sturdy garden flat or any shallow wood box; plastic bag; trowel; potting soil; aquarium pebbles; myrtle seedlings; creeping thyme; miniature ornament.

easter

sunday

Pussy willow wands, bowls of pansies, and straw hats garnished with fresh tulips and daffodils set the stage for an old-fashioned Easter at the farmhouse, where nature provides the color for most decorations. Each year, preparations begin the week before Easter Sunday, when redware and wood darning eggs and a collection of tissue-covered ornaments from the 1940s are nested into pretty baskets. James also makes traditional Easter decorations, dying dozens of farm eggs (white or brown) a rich mahogany by simmering them for three or four hours in a dye made with water, vinegar, and yellow and red onion skins.

At the Easter dinner table, a small pot of miniature jonquils marks each place. After the blooms have faded, these are transplanted outdoors, where they multiply and bloom again the following year. At sunrise on Easter morning, James can be found in the greenhouse, happily filling straw hats with a fluffy mixture of potting soil and peat moss. Into these he tucks plenty of fresh herbs, flowers, and decorated eggs to create living Easter baskets that are fleeting in their beauty, yet filled with the promise of spring.

A shoebox unearthed at a flea market yielded these tissue-covered eggs, blown out and delicately trimmed in the 1940s. Here they nestle in a painted basket (lined with a plastic bag) on a bed of flax. Scattered on moist potting soil, the seeds sprout within a week; a daily spritz of water keeps the greenery lush.

Festive table decorations proclaim the arrival of spring. Oversized carrots made from old wool scraps (above left) recall the velvet fruit and vegetable decorations popular in the 1930s. A wooden tray displays redware eggs (above right) and an overturned straw hat whose crown harbors a fluffy nest of candytuft blooms and a redware bunny and chicks (right).

Hats filled with thyme and dotted
with spring flowers (left) make nests
for quails' eggs; the fabric rooster,
chicken, and carrots were hand–hooked
by a friend. Painted wooden darning
eggs, shiny from years of service,
nestle into a hat full of violas trimmed
with miniature daffodils (below left).
Sewn from linen, the perching
bird has wings and tail of pleated
paper (below right).

herb-covered eggs

Foam eggs rolled in aromatic spices and herbs combine the charm of Easter eggs with the spicy fragrance of old-fashioned pomanders. Materials and equipment: Styrofoam eggs in any size (available at crafts shops); white glue; shallow bowl; fragrant spices such as allspice, cinnamon, and ground cloves; orrisroot (a fixative to preserve scent); newspaper; dried lavender; bay leaves; pressed or dried flowers; hot glue gun (optional).

A. Cover a Styrofoam egg with white glue, rubbing it on with your hands. In a shallow bowl, add the spices, mixing them in whatever proportions you like. Add 1 tablespoon of orrisroot.

B. While the glue is still wet, gently roll the egg in the spice mixture, being careful not to smear the glue. When the egg is well coated with spice, set it aside on a piece of newspaper and let it dry for a day or two.

C. Draw a ring of glue around the center of the egg lengthwise and roll the egg in the lavender. Glue two or three bay leaves to the side of the egg and add a pressed or dried flower.

S U M

Trim the boxwood, fill the birdbaths, water the garden, and weed, weed, weed. That, in short, is summer at Seven Gates Farm. The unofficial high point of the season is the Fourth of July, when Dean displays his collection of hand-stitched American flags and fireworks illuminate the night sky over the Civil War battlefields just down the road at Antietam.

A crab festival is another tradition ~ a happy gathering of friends who spend a long, lazy afternoon dining on this famous Maryland delicacy, along with mountains of shrimp and corn on the cob. ✒ But the real glory of the season is found in small moments and ordinary pastimes:

M E R

grooming topiaries still fresh with early-morning  dew; drinking coffee on the front porch as the traffic on South Main Street quickens; spending a rainy afternoon in the house, a quiet sanctuary whose interiors are pared down to bare floors and cool linens. ❧ Although these seasonal pleasures endure, the farm has continued to change. In the gardens, there are more flowers and herbs and fewer vegetables than a decade ago; busy lives necessitate more self-sufficient plantings. James and Dean have also redesigned the  washhouse, now a cool retreat. On summer days, they often escape here to sip a refreshing drink and discuss new projects for the weeks ahead. ❧

in the

gardens

Plucked from the tree, leaves and all, ripe peaches fill a forked-twig basket (opposite). Large topiaries (four and five years old) hover around the smokehouse terrace (overleaf) like guests at a garden party. To make the terrace, stones from the property were set in a circle and linked with a carpet of fragrant creeping thyme transplanted from the nearby herb garden. Hummingbirds flock to the showy trumpet vine, which threatens to overtake the smokehouse roof no matter how often it is cut back.

If spring is the season of anticipation at Seven Gates Farm, summer is the reward. The gardens are mature; spring cleaning is done and most beds need only routine maintenance such as deadheading, watering, and, of course, endless weeding.

The backbone of the flower gardens are the perennials, which provide a natural sequence of color as new blossoms unfold just when others are beginning to fade. Among the first to show its welcome face is a clematis vine, a flowering climber that comes back strong each May after taking a tentative hold on a rustic bench in the white garden several years ago. Traditional favorites appear throughout the remainder of the season, among them daisies (early June), followed by mounds of orange day lilies around the topiary garden (July), and cone flowers in the white garden (August). Some plants bloom at the start of summer and again late in the season, while others, including white iceberg roses growing near the smokehouse, flourish all summer and even into October. "I plant them because they are *easy,* and they always look fresh," says James.

A birdhouse sprinkler ~ a hose is attached in back ~ sends a cooling fan of water over day lilies, silver artemesia, yellow coreopsis, and mint (below left). Dryer quarters are provided by a log-cabin birdhouse (below right) bought from a roadside stand on a visit to Tennessee; nailed to a tree limb, it stands amid a bed of orange mint.

The sheer variety of flowers, shrubs, and other vines ~ and the contrast in scale and texture they provide ~ brings interest to the summer landscape. Lush vines scale roofs and arbors to draw the eye upward. Manicured topiaries provide a polite counterpoint to untamed flower beds. Evergreens establish a look of permanence and espaliered pear trees "join hands" to create a fence by the vegetable garden, where lettuce (sown from seeds, plucked, and replanted all summer) sprouts from raised beds. And, perhaps most important, a host of birdhouses, scarecrows, jaunty signs, and rustic garden furnishings lend the yard an irresistible sense of whimsy and fun.

attracting birds

Country dwellers know that birds delight both eye and ear; they swoop and sing, teach their wobbly young to fly ~ and they also dine on insects, making them ideal tenants for yard and garden. Although particular species are said to favor particular houses, Dean recommends a less studied approach: "I just put up a house and see what comes." The surprise tenants in his ornate Victorian-era martin house, for example, were three families of starlings; the expected martins were never able to move in.

It is best to place any birdhouse in a sheltered spot, high enough to keep cats at bay. Birds will not nest where they sense danger, so if a house remains unoccupied for more than a summer or two, move it. The birds usually tend to housekeeping themselves, although washing a birdhouse with boiling water very early in the spring gives nesters a clean start. To make your yard even more hospitable to winged visitors, provide a variety of feeders, fresh water, and shrubs and trees for roosting.

A woven flower cone from Tennessee holds fresh-picked blossoms (near right). On the table (far right) are pots of white zinnias that bloom all summer long. James found a single climbing rose bush struggling to survive in the middle of the yard and transplanted it to the kitchen garden (below) where it thrives, flowering in early June. The fence encloses herb beds and a yard for Elijah the dog; a screened porch is eventually planned for this spot.

Antique clothing is hung to air on a twig-braced clothesline (above). Just behind the house, transplanted grapevines are trained over a grape arbor (left). The trellised roof is made of three long branches with shorter branches placed crosswise. A riot of color, the former potpourri garden (overleaf) is now the site of a formal white garden.

rustic twig scarecrow

A. Saw a tree limb for the body. (This one is 18 inches long and 4 inches in diameter.) For the face, remove an 8-inch section of bark by scoring in circles with a chisel, then peeling the bark with a penknife. Drill a ½-inch diameter hole 2 inches deep into the body top.

B. Cut small nose and eye pieces from tree branches and nail in place. Chisel out the mouth. Using tin snips, cut a bow-tie shape from tin. Cut a log piece for the hat crown; drill a ½-inch diameter hole 2 inches deep in the base of the crown. Cut a 4-inch length of ½-inch dowel.

C. For the hat brim, cut tin into a circle (about 9 inches in diameter). Drill a ½-inch diameter hole in the center. Fit the hat dowel into the log crown, then slide on the tin brim. Fit the free end of the dowel into the log body and slide the pieces together until they fit snugly.

D. Cut arms from twigs. With the penknife, whittle one end of each twig flat on one side and nail it to the body; predrill nail holes in the twigs if the arms seem likely to split. Nail on the bow tie. Drill a ¾-inch diameter hole in the base of the body for the stand.

Not all scarecrows have to chase birds; some just look great in the garden. Dean makes his dignified stick men from apple or peach boughs. Hat brims and ties are cut from galvanized tin, sold at salvage yards; a can lid or tarpaper are fine, too. Edward Toolhands (above), has hands made from old tool heads. For safety, clamp wood pieces to a worktable before cutting and drilling. Round all corners of tin. Materials and equipment: saw; tree limbs and sticks; wood chisel; penknife; drill; 1¼-inch nails; hammer; tin snips; sheet tin; ½-inch dowel (4 inches long for hat); ¾-inch dowel (4 feet long for stand).

the vegetable

"There is nothing as sweet as that first homegrown tomato."

garden

Although the men plant marigolds in the vegetable garden each year ~ the sharp fragrance is said to deter trespassing wildlife ~ Dean's board fence (opposite) probably does more to keep animals out; the sign was a gift from a friend. By midsummer, the garden is at its peak, peaceful and lush (overleaf). Conventional wisdom holds that vegetables be well-spaced, but James plants tight rows that he can reach from either side. He found he can grow more in a smaller area and the plants do just as well.

Each year the vegetable garden starts out neat and orderly, but by summer it's in full sprawl. Rambunctious squash vines send their curious tendrils everywhere, the bush beans are bushy, and broccoli bouquets flourish. In June, onions and peas sown in early March and potatoes buried on St. Patrick's Day for good luck are about ready to harvest. This bounty is a triumph of man over nature; because the plot was once part of a horse pasture, it has a fairly rich soil, but the hard clay must still be reworked each growing season. To prepare the beds, James uses vintage garden tools ~ many from the 1920s and 1930s. His one concession to modern technology is a new rototiller.

Much of James's gardening know-how, he says, was learned at the knee of his Aunt Ruth, who planted a huge vegetable garden each year until she was well into her nineties. His own plot at Seven Gates, however, measures a compact 20-by-20 feet. "We found that for us, a large garden was a waste because we couldn't use it all," he confesses. "So we cut back and only plant what we really enjoy." To make the most of the space, Dean built a trio of raised beds using treated

Paths spread with straw to keep weeds down separate thriving rows of onions, zucchini, and beans and provide access to raised beds. The lush foliage of gourds and cucumbers serves as an umbrella for the strawberries underneath.

2-by-6 foot lumber at one end of the garden. Packed with well-composted soil, the beds soak up moisture and offer ideal conditions for cucumbers, strawberries, gourds, and herbs. The open area beyond is reserved for sprawlers like squash, peas, and bush beans, and rows of tomato plants, which are surrounded by straw so the fruit won't fall in the dirt when branches droop with a ripe crop.

While the plots are filled with old standbys, it is also a tradition to add something new each year. One season, it was scarlet runner-bean seeds, a gift from a friend. Another, it was white pumpkins with seeds saved from some bought the previous fall. There have been failed experiments, too, begun in earnest and regretfully abandoned. For James, it was artichokes, which need a longer growing season than Keedysville could offer.

A denim-clad scarecrow built by Dean oversees the tomato patch (above left); James made the rustic twig sign. Hollyhocks rise against the trellis, crafted from weathered tree limbs and hung with hollowed bottle gourds (above right), which are favored by nesting wrens. Tin garden markers (left) are fanciful reminders.

James and Dean spent one Memorial
Day weekend building a pine
potting shed from plans sketched on
a whim. The cedar-shingled
cupola (right) sports a trowel finial
and curved vents inspired by
similar details on 18th-century well
houses in Williamsburg, Virginia.
Wild jasmine, which will bloom in the
autumn, climbs a trellis made from
old chair rockers (below left). The free-
form door wreath is actually an old
handmade sprinkler, while the recycled
rose head of a watering can spout
makes a fine doorknob (below right).

The "plants" sign (left) was snapped
up at a flea market in Maryland;
when the shed was pictured in
a magazine, a woman wrote to James
and Dean saying she had sold the
sign twelve years ago at a yard sale
in Pennsylvania. Whitewashed
walls silhouette antique tools and a
miniature trellis (above).

the white

garden

Clipped paths and symmetrical beds lend a gentle sense of formality to the white garden, an oasis of calm on a swath of lawn just north of the house. White had always played a part in these beds, but a few years ago James succumbed to a growing urge to give the one color a leading role. "White gardens are calming," he says, "and I prefer white flowers in bouquets."

Transplanting everything that wasn't white or a shade of green to other gardens, James began anew. In came loads of tall wavy cleomes, pale mounds of pearly everlasting, meandering white clematis, white tulips, dahlias, and phlox ~ there are some 20 varieties of annuals and perennials growing here now. To set off the white flowers he designed a framework of dwarf evergreens and deciduous shrubs; a row of boxwoods and hydrangea trees forms a border and corner fences define the square layout. A strong design, says James, is important because it ensures the garden looks good throughout the year, especially off season. In fact, when snow caps the boxwood, junipers, and holly and dusts the boughs of evergreens, the white garden truly lives up to its name.

James starts cleomes from seeds in the greenhouse and uses them for tall accents. The wavy stamens have earned this striking annual the nickname "spider flower"; huge heads reach four and five feet high (opposite). A bird's-eye view of the white garden (overleaf) shows off its formal, symmetrical composition. The border of boxwoods and hydrangea trees is new and will fill out with time. The interior flower beds, now replanted in an all-white scheme, are holdovers from an earlier potpourri garden.

In its first life, the white garden
was planted with red roses and purple
lavender (right), used for making
potpourri. James was ready to throw
away the old twig bench, but a
bold clematis vine had already gained
a foothold, turning the back into
a trellis. Three years later, the garden
was all white and the bench fully
covered (below), joined by a white-
blooming chamomile bush and two
potted dwarf spruces moved from their
sheltered winter posts on the porch.

white garden plants

Alyssum

Candytuft

Chamomile

Clematis

Cleome

Cone Flower

Dahlia

Florence White Cornflower

Hydrangea

Iceberg Rose

Lavender (white)

Marigold

Nicotiana

Pearly Everlasting

Phlox

Pincushion Flower

Roma Lily

Silver Lace Vine

Snowlady Shasta Daisy

Star White Zinnia

Tulip

Wax Begonia

A metal arbor covered with a tangle of silver lace vine, frames the garden entrance (top). The centerpiece, and first shrub to bloom in spring, is a star magnolia (above) circled by a stone path and framed by mounds of pearly everlasting; cedar chips help keep weeds at bay.

the green

house

Rain spatters the ribbed windows of the greehouse on a summer day. Inside is a quiet still life of upturned English flowerpots with large drainage holes; when James bought them, they reminded him of miniature rhubarb forcers. The painted wire plant stand from the Victorian era was an unexpected find on a trip through a Maryland antiques emporium.

By the end of June, the greenhouse takes on its summer guise. Emptied of most of its spring trappings, the structure shows off its handsome bones. Seedlings started back in February and March have outgrown the need for shelter and are now acclimating themselves to permanent homes in the herb and vegetable gardens. Iron garden chairs, which frequently shuttle outdoors for summer picnics, pose like mannequins on the bed of river pebbles covering the floor. A birdhouse and a cloche or two sit on bare potting benches, like artworks in a gallery. And there is a precise appeal to the neat rows of staked topiaries, lined up side by side.

As these, the youngest topiaries, still need shelter, they remain inside the greenhouse throughout the summer and the following winter. Any myrtles larger than golf-ball size, however, are moved to the terrace by the smokehouse so they can gain strength from a summer outdoors. "This is very good for house plants, too," declares James. "The longer any potted plants are out, the healthier they are ~ and they're going to do better in your house when you bring them back inside in the fall."

Quiet as a schoolhouse during
summer vacation, the greenhouse
becomes a showcase for soldierly rows
of topiaries and other potted plants.
A charmingly down-at-the-heels
1930s garden chair (above) is one of
a pair that serve as handy plant
stands; wax begonias, which James
propagates from cuttings, spill
out of a painted wood box. Hanging
baskets hold creeping figs (right)
that were unhappy in the house but
thrive in the hot, humid climate
here. To temper the beating Maryland
sun, James drapes the roof peak
with a single length of burlap, tied
in place at each end and laid in
soft folds over the metal cross beams.

house

Among the features that first attracted James and Dean to their property were the sturdy old out-buildings, with so many tales to tell of everyday life on this 19th-century working farm. Here, in the venerable timber-framed washhouse, built shortly after the 1830s farmhouse, huge pots of water were boiled in the fireplace every Monday, the traditional laundry day. The building also served as a summer kitchen: When it was too hot to cook in the main house, meals were prepared over the vast open hearth. Even today, opening the front and side doors welcomes a cooling breeze that was surely appreciated as much then as it is now.

In the men's first years here, the washhouse stored baskets, antiques picked up at markets and shows, and Dean's birdhouses. It was also used for drying herbs, flower, and other plants James makes into decorations and potpourri; the dry, dark interior was ideal for this. Eventually, however, the structure became overcrowded and lost its original simplicity. So James and Dean decided to clear out their belongings and recast the old washhouse as a summer kitchen ~ not for cooking, this time, but as a pleasant place to cool off and relax.

Sheathed with lapped German siding, the washhouse probably dates to around the 1840s. Covering an upper-level window, a martin house offers eight doors to visiting birds. The rustic gate, made from sycamore branches, is overgrown with oregano.

99

Herbs and flowers are best dried in a well-ventilated spot, away from direct sunlight. To support the flower heads of large-blossomed plants like allium, James suspends them in a drying rack; this simple homemade device consists of nothing more than a piece of chicken wire bent over two twigs.

good plants for drying

Allium

Bush Bean

Chive Blossom

Hydrangea

Lamb's Ear

Larkspur

Lavender

Lemon Verbena

Marjoram

Mint

Oregano

Pearly Everlasting

Peony

Rosemary

Rose

Sage

Santolina

Silver King Artemesia

Thyme

Queen Anne's Lace

Yarrow

A new coat of whitewash was splashed onto the walls, fireplace, and beams, and the furnishings were reduced to just a few basic pieces that suited the space: an old hutch table, a few ladderback chairs, and a sturdy stepback cupboard that had once stood in the kitchen. James still dries herbs here, but not nearly as much as he once did; now, there is plenty of room to sit with friends who drop in for conversation and refreshment.

On a summer day when it's raining outside and the door and windows are thrown wide open, the washhouse is especially inviting. Its simplicity calms the soul.

A primitive drying rack from the Shenandoah Valley holds a supply of artemesia (above left); fresh-picked blossoms fill the field basket. James recommends drying heavy-headed flowers upside down so that the blooms don't droop (above right). These yellow roses dangle from single pieces of jute to let air circulate; bunching flowers together will break the leaves.

Refurnished as a summer sitting room, the 12-by-12-foot washhouse interior is the perfect place for an evening glass of wine. Airy linens pinned to a length of clothesline camouflage the black-painted fireplace interior. Sculptural scythes and a swag of dried lily blossoms and lemon leaves decorate the chimney breast. To pave the floor, James and Dean removed the old boards, leveled the dirt base with sand, then laid a layer of new, seasoned bricks. More sand was poured into the joints and the excess swept away; no mortar was used.

scented waters

The idea began simply enough. It was a hot summer day, guests were coming, and James and Dean wanted the washhouse to look cool and inviting. They set a yellowware bowl on the table, filled it with fresh spring water, then cast a handful of lemon rinds and mint leaves afloat. The sight was so refreshing, no one could resist dipping in their fingers.

Bowls of scented water, which hold all the restorative charms of a pool in miniature, have now become a signature of summer at Seven Gates. They are found not only in the washhouse, but also in the kitchen, bathroom, and on the terrace, where birds sometimes alight for a closer look ~ and even an occasional sip. Lime (slices or rinds), sage leaves, rosemary, rose petals, and violets all look and smell equally enticing floating in a pretty bowl. A drop of rose water or essential oil will enhance the scent indoors.

The window box overflows with dahlias, silver thyme, salmon flocks-of-sheep (grown from English seeds), ivy, and white violas (opposite). Working the soil well before planting and fertilizing regularly keeps box planters like this lush. The lean-to (left) stores garden tools and firewood. Original framing timbers are exposed inside (below left); knotted cheesecloth makes an airy summer curtain (below right).

in the

house

Hung on a homemade hanger, a child's cotton smock stitched in the 1870s is a backdrop for an exuberant bouquet of hydrangeas and yarrow plucked from the white garden and gathered in a McCoy pottery cachepot (opposite). Creamy linen pillows come out of storage to replace winter wools on the sofa (overleaf); other living room decorations are pared down to a few simple accessories such as the string balls ~ looking cool as snowballs ~ piled in a painted dough box. The front door is thrown open so the living room and porch become one airy, free-flowing space.

Bare wood floors, wide-open doors, and armloads of cut flowers: Readied for the season, the farmhouse is "dressed down" for the slow, hot months of summer.

By July, James and Dean are taking full advantage of the long hours of daylight and spend most of their time outside, puttering lazily in the gardens, relaxing on their front porch, or lingering over meals on the back terrace. The interior of the house, in turn, becomes a cool retreat.

Downstairs floors are scrubbed, while rag rugs in upstairs bedrooms are put away and sisal mats rolled out in their place. James, who prefers to leave things unframed, is apt to just pin up a few interesting items wherever he sees fit, which perfectly suits the offhand summer mood of the interiors. Cloth seed bags might be displayed on a plain plaster wall or a paper quilt pattern tacked to a bit of old board propped casually on a mantelpiece. A few accessories do remain ~ a piece of antique clothing draped on a chair back, perhaps, or a miniature log cabin left by itself on a table ~ but the carefully arranged collections that warm up the rooms in colder months are now temporarily tucked out of sight behind closed cupboard doors.

*James loves the glamorous look
of full-blown roses. Cut lots,
he advises, and pack them tightly.
Mint sprigs peek out from a
cluster of antique climbing roses
(above left); catching the afternoon
sun, the bouquet is shown off
in a 1930s pitcher (above right).*

"With less on display," explains James, "the house is much easier to take care of, and it feels cooler, too."

Summer is, instead, the season for natural decorations: Oversize bouquets of cut flowers from the gardens take center stage in every room of the house. These lovely, free-spirited arrangements are James's specialty and he credits their appeal to the beauty of the plants themselves. "In fact, I don't really arrange flowers," he claims. "It's more that I try to re-create the effect they have when they are growing outdoors." A casual mass of snowy blossoms from the white garden, for example, looks as cool as hankies blowing in the breeze. Herbs ~ plenty of them ~ are also mixed in with the flowers; among

James's favorites are fragrant mint, basil, and lemon balm, which add their own scents to the summer mix. Garden vegetables, too, are singled out for their intriguing shapes and mellow glow, and included in a basket of flowers or simply set on a table beside it.

James also favors unusual containers, which might be just about anything that holds water: 1930s cachepots and pitchers, a battered tin watering can, old thermoses, vintage seed jars. Even if an improvised vase can't hold water on its own, it probably can camouflage a jar or can of water inside ~ which is how the old berry and picnic baskets collected at Seven Gates Farm also come to be brimming with lush summer blooms.

A green-painted basket stuffed with a jar of sage, pink-blooming oregano, and zucchini makes a casual table centerpiece (below left). A twig pedestal holds a pitcher of Shasta daisies and lemon balm, mingled with pink flowers snipped from a carpet of blooming ground cover with heart-shaped leaves (below right.)

Delicate herbs and flowers, including nasturtium, dill weed, Queen Anne's lace, and sweet peas, fill old seed jars with their original labels; some country stores still sell seeds in bulk from containers like these. For the prettiest effect, James parades old jars and bottles in a single line. They go almost anywhere: on a mantelpiece, window sill, shelf, or even across the seat of a vacated porch swing.

At least one summer day at Seven Gates Farm is always devoted to making flavored vinegars, which are shown off in interesting wine and water bottles ~ many picked up at flea markets ~ sterilized with boiling water. Left to steep in a sunny window for several weeks, wine vinegars flavored with herbs transform themselves into tasty dressings to splash on salads, meat, fish, and chicken, and to present as holiday gifts.

summer vinegars

Flavored summer vinegars steeped in pretty glass jars and bottles are as lovely to look at as they are pleasing to the palate. To make them, James and Dean put a few fresh-snipped herbs in a clean container and fill it with white-wine vinegar. The container should stand for two weeks so the vinegar can soak up the flavors of the contents. Favorite recipes from Seven Gates Farm:

- chive blossoms and tarragon

- silver thyme sprigs, black peppercorns, and torn nasturtium blossoms

- chives, whole chive blossoms, dill sprigs, and black peppercorns

- rosemary and peeled garlic cloves

- dill sprigs, chopped garlic, and red pepper flakes

- white garlic-chive blossoms and chopped garlic

*A Tennessee feed bin serves as a
kitchen work island (above);
the antique portable desktop resting
on it props cookbooks. The open
door leads to the kitchen garden, the
private domain of Elijah the dog.
James's collection of velvet strawberry
pincushions from the Victorian era,
piled into vintage farmstand baskets,
gather on a homespun runner (left).*

Atop the work island (opposite), a melon basket is filled with duck eggs. Over the sink is a green-painted spice box and apothecary jars filled with dried herbs from the garden. The kitchen fireplace (above) is decorated with a string of fresh herb bundles; these bouquets of sage and oregano will stay fragrant for weeks. Sharing space with impatiens in antique pots, a paper quilt pattern decorates the dining room mantel for summer (left).

*In the second-story stair hall (opposite)
black rag dolls gather on the seat
of a red-painted hutch table; a linsey-
woolsey quilt hangs over the upended
top. Inspired by the bare spots left
when old linoleum (tacked down like
rugs) was taken up, James simply
painted in stencils and borders
to make trompe l'oeil carpets. In the
northeast bedroom, homespun is
the theme; a late 19th-century dress
poses on a dressmakers' form (left);
the pillowcases are new, made to
match an antique comforter (below).*

the fourth

"*Independence deserves to be celebrated.*"

# of july

Independence Day is commemorated in grand style at Seven Gates Farm. Flags fly, buntings and banners unfurl, and the house is decked out in red, white, and blue. For Dean and James, the Fourth is a day to celebrate the birth of the nation and the independence they, too, enjoy as self-employed artists and craftsmen.

The centerpiece of the holiday decoration, the flags are part of a collection Dean started ten years ago, when he focused a lifelong interest in textiles on this specialized field. A Civil War buff since childhood, he often visited forts and battlefields with his father in their home state of Tennessee. Keedysville is just down the road from Antietam, where in 1862 the bloodiest single day of the Civil War was fought, so patriotic memorabilia is everywhere in the area. Old American flags, however, are difficult to find because many were burned or lost to weather and war. Those that survive are fragile, often passed form collector to collector without ever reaching the open market. To date, Dean's best find may be a flag he discovered in Tennessee: Made in 1900, it was stitched by Rachel Albright, the 90-year-old granddaughter of Betsy Ross.

On the Fouth of July, every detail counts. Antique miniature flags and delicate iceberg roses peek from the pocket of a pair of children's overalls dated to about 1920. The hand-stitched calico shirt was made at the turn of the century.

*Hail Old Glory! A flag flies
from a pole that once stood
at the old Hagerstown, Maryland,
fairgrounds; Dean found it
in Virginia and brought it back
to its home state. A banner
from an 1866 veteran's reunion
decorates the front door. The
oldest bunting, hung over the front
step, dates to the 19th century.*

125

*A highlight of a finely crafted
Civil War–era flag from
the Philadelphia area (above)
is its blue wool canton with
a rare Double Wreath pattern of
35 stars. A few crude stitches
suggest the flag may have been
damaged during battle and
hastily repaired (right).*

Children made these flaglets (left) to wave at Civil War–era parades and rallies; embroidered Xs serve as stars. A rare 1863 flag from New Hampshire (below left) has a Great Star pattern, which was popular from about 1818 through the Civil War. The blue chintz canton was "polished" with egg whites to produce a sheen. Thirteen hand-sewn stars adorn an 1847 cloth-covered shield (below right), originally used at political gatherings.

COLLECTING
calicoes

Nothing bespeaks the spirit of country quite like calico, the dainty-print cottons so synonymous with early American life. Although calico evokes images of prairies and pioneers, it is not native to this country. Printed cottons originated in India hundreds of years ago and derive their name from Calicut, a major port on the Malabar Coast. Shipped out by the British East India Company, calicoes ~ which included white and solid-color fabrics as well as hand prints ~ were available in America as early as the 1600s.

The hand-blocked fabric was expensive, however, and it was not until the mid-19th century that advancements in textile printing and dye techniques made commercially printed cotton yardage an affordable alternative to homespun linen and wool. It was also around this time that the small prints now traditionally thought of as calico became prevalent.

The naïve innocence and gaiety of calico pinafores, aprons, and doll clothes draw enthusiastic admirers today. James's collection includes garments made for children and for adults in the late 19th and early 20th centuries. Blue calicoes dyed with indigo are easiest to find; early brown dyes contained acids that cause cotton to deteriorate. There is no need to pass up an item just because the condition isn't perfect, however. Patches and wear give a piece character, a down-home feeling, and a welcome sense of history.

A U T

Fall is a season of reckoning at Seven Gates Farm, when James and Dean reappraise the yard and make changes accordingly. (One year, it was a new color scheme: The red fence around the property was repainted green, and the tin roofs on the old outbuildings, also red, were toned down with black.) ✿ Seeds are saved and cloches set out in the gardens where they protect plants from early frosts, help ripen the last squash, and shelter parsley so it can be enjoyed

fresh all winter long. Daffodil and tulip bulbs are tucked into pots for forcing, and geraniums, ivy, and topiaries that have summered outdoors take their new places in the house and

U   M   N

greenhouse. Pumpkins and gourds, always paired for the best effect, replace plants in outdoor urns, and bittersweet is gathered for door and mantel  arrangements. ❧ James and Dean spend the mild days of Indian summer taking Elijah the dog for long walks. In the process, they almost always stumble on something wonderful to delight the eye: acorn-laden branches destined to become a lush Thanksgiving wreath, perhaps, or colorful leaves used to wrap gift preserves. Maryland is apple country, and as the days start to

 grow short, the two men make a final trip to local farmstands to stock up on baskets of Macouns, sweet apple butter, and gallons of pressed cider. ❧

in the

"*The flower beds bloom one last time before another year comes to a close.*"

gardens

Autumn at Seven Gates is a gratifying time in the gardens, which regain some of their good looks for a month or two. By mid-September the parching weather has passed and bright yellow fall crocuses begin to poke up by the front porch. Spent annuals and herbs cut back by James in late summer "green up" again until the first frost cuts them short. Leaves are raked, then chopped fine with a chipper to make a rich mulch that is spread an all beds. This is especially important on the north side of the house, where ferns and hostas need extra protection during the winter. The vegetable garden also receives a helping of leaf mulch after the plot is cleared out and a few last vegetables are sown, including garlic for spring harvesting and spinach and turnips to be enjoyed in late fall. "The tradition of turnips comes from my Aunt Ruth," notes James, who plants these hearty root vegetables in October. "You just take a handful of seeds and pitch them out," he explains. "Wherever they fall, they come up. They're ready in 30 days and love the cold; I pick turnips right up until Christmas."

Fall leaves weave a colorful carpet for the white garden, where evergreens frame a strong design after the flowers have faded (opposite). A bordering row of young boxwoods continues into the lawn creating an outdoor room (overleaf); the "entry" is flanked by concrete finials that once topped brick pillars at the entrance to a Virginia estate. The tall evergreens in the background had a former life as balled-root Christmas trees. James digs holes for them in autumn before the ground freezes, then plants the trees in January, insulating their roots with leaf mulch.

Virtually anything gathered from yard, garden, woods, and farmstand seems to work together naturally for autumn decorations. On a pine farm table, a windswept scattering of leaves, apples, and pears shows the season's bounty. The pumpkins and small acorn finials are wood; the larger wood sculpture is a decorative folk carving of indeterminate age.

Autumn is also the time when spring- and summer-blooming perennials are lifted and divided to propagate the plants and ensure their good health; most are divided every two or three years. James leaves some of the faded perennial flowers for the birds, but cuts back the rest. When annuals die out, he saves the seeds from the flower heads; these are dried in paper bags, and stored in glass jars until spring. In the place of summer plants, eye-catching arrangements of harvest fare ~ Indian corn; white and salmon pumpkins remarkable for their soft, ethereal hues; and corn stalks ~ now bring interest to the yard. And as autumn fades into winter, the two men stock up on fresh plants to renew planters and urns: evergreens, boxwood, and fall pansies that continue to bloom even through winter snows.

Bittersweet, pumpkins, and dried sunflowers are congenial autumn companions. One large sunflower head (left) yields dozens of seeds, which are shared with birds. A pair of enormous pumpkins (below), made of white-painted cedar, mimic real ones of the Lumina variety.

By the washhouse, stark black-eyed
Susans gone to seed form a hedge
of moody color (left); the border of sage
and santolina in front looks good
long after the rest of the gardens have
faded. The window box is filled
with pansies, vinca, and decorative
cabbage plants, which are fall tenants
only. Sheltering trees and a board-
and-batten birdhouse mounted high
on a post make this corner of the
garden (above) highly attractive to
winged visitors.

141

The herb garden (above) is still
colorful in the fall, with parsley and
thyme for the picking. If the weather
is good, potted topiaries can stay
outdoors until mid-October. A spray
of bittersweet adds a flourish of
color to the potting-shed door (right).
James planted this tenacious vine
by the back porch ten years ago
and has since divided and replanted
it by Dean's workshop and the
smokehouse fence.

*After a rainstorm, a stone
watering trough from England
becomes a reflecting pool filled
with fall leaves (left); although it's
too high for Elijah the Yorkie,
neighborhood dogs and cats use it
as a watering stop on evening patrols.
The smokehouse terrace (below)
is a pleasant place to gather on a
warm Indian summer day; the
cozy-looking plaid wool blanket is
from James's working collection of
antique homespun textiles.*

Scarecrow men hovering amid
the garnet blossoms of sedum Autumn
Joy look more like a friendly
welcoming committee than a posse
of bird chasers. Gigantic striped
squash are heaped in the foreground;
the piles flank a rambling growth of
southernwood, a fragrant herb
traditionally used as a moth repellent.

Most plants from the garden find more than one use at Seven Gates. Slices of baby pumpkin hang on an oak apple dryer (right), destined for autumn potpourri. On the back porch, dried bush beans, which are known as leather britches in the South, are strung with needle and thread to make a whimsical curtain (below). James saves the seeds for spring planting.

a harvest of gourds

Bottle gourds, a hearty variety of climbing vine named for the slender necks of the fruit, are among the easiest members of the gourd family to raise. For an extended crop, seeds should be planted early in spring as weather permits; they can also be started indoors in peat pots, then transplanted, pot and all, to the base of a fence or trellis when danger of frost is past. After the fall harvest, Dean hangs the gourds by the crooks of their necks in a warm, dry place. By spring, the outer skins have flaked off and the gourds are dry (the seeds rattle inside). To make birdhouses, which recall a Native American tradition, he uses a penknife to cut an entry hole (half-dollar size for martins, quarter-size for wrens), then gently drills a hole in the neck and suspends the gourd from a tree limb or pole with string or wire. Martins prefer a perch of 15 to 20 feet high; a lower station invites wrens.

Corn stalks bunched and tied around
the flagpole (right) are an autumn
tradition. Other outdoor arrangements
constantly change. One year, for
example, a single Halloween pumpkin
on a bed of straw and trailing vinca
filled a cast-iron urn (below left);
the next year, a variety of gourds and
white pumpkins took their place
(below right). A vine-entwined twig
chair makes a natural display
stand for more pumpkins (opposite).

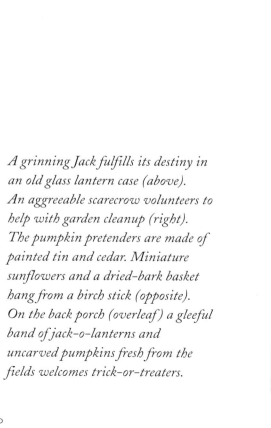

*A grinning Jack fulfills its destiny in
an old glass lantern case (above).
An aggreeable scarecrow volunteers to
help with garden cleanup (right).
The pumpkin pretenders are made of
painted tin and cedar. Miniature
sunflowers and a dried-bark basket
hang from a birch stick (opposite).
On the back porch (overleaf) a gleeful
band of jack-o-lanterns and
uncarved pumpkins fresh from the
fields welcomes trick-or-treaters.*

gift preserves

Wrapped snugly with simple, natural trims from the garden, jars of home preserves and store-bought specialty foods make engaging gifts and are also pretty just sitting on a windowsill or grouped as part of an autumn centerpiece. Maple leaves (below) and corn husks (opposite) are good choices; James also uses squash, hosta, and dogwood leaves. Materials and equipment: leaves and corn husks; twine, raffia, or string; scissors.

A. Gather large, fresh green leaves or autumn leaves that are still pliable. Corn husks may be used dry or green. If the leaves seem brittle, gently rinse them in water so they are soft enough to bend without breaking.

B. Gently place the husks or leaves (veins down) over the jar lid; use one, or overlap in twos or threes, depending on their size. Bend the edges over the rim; with your free hand, wrap twine around the jar lid once or twice and tie to secure.

C. Set the jar aside in a dry, well-ventilated place. Green leaves and husks will "cure" naturally, drying to fit the lid.

house

By October, the farmhouse is dressed for autumn. Twigs collected from the yard stoke a huge kindling basket by the kitchen fireplace. Bundles of dried rosemary are laid on the hearth and will soon be tossed on a blazing fire to release their rich aroma into the air. The dining room fireplace, rarely used, is filled to overflowing with pine cones, and fall pansies, snug in terra-cotta pots, are tucked around the house to offer tiny reprises of spring.

At this time of year, James always has a pocket full of acorns, his favorite nuts for decorating. He uses them as finishing touches amid the pumpkins, fruit, and flowers that are scattered on tables and plant stands in every room. "It looks like a squirrel lives here," says Dean with a laugh. Both men are particularly fond of the collections that come out of summer storage at this time of year: The stuffed black-sock cats, rag dolls, hooked rugs, and quilts bought at sales in Keedysville seem to suit their house so well. Other pieces may come and go as their collections grow and change, but James and Dean claim these locally made treasures finally have found a permanent home at Seven Gates.

Set off by a basket, a green transferware plate made in the 1880s becomes the focal point of a mantel display when its pattern is highlighted by accessories from the wild, including gourds, a Seckel pear, maple leaves, and a beige pumpkin. The beeswax ear-of-corn candle is pierced on a painted tin candlestick.

157

A covey of soft fabric birds in fall regalia feathers its nests with pine cones and acorns on the kitchen mantel (below). The hooked rug, made in 1890, was purchased locally. Once used to warm floorboards, it is now preserved as an effective wall display.

In the kitchen (opposite), the stillness of an autumn afternoon is captured by a brilliant spray of sage and maple leaves tucked in a wood firkin. The hanging meat rack, with hooks made of dogwood branches, came from a smokehouse in Petersburg, Virginia.

Year-old gourds with their tops
sawn off hold smaller gourds and a
potpourri of sage, fall leaves,
lemon verbena, and dried pumpkin
slices (above left). Corn stalks
and tassels pop from a flowering
cabbage, planted in a hollow
pumpkin filled with soil (above right).
A turn-of-the-century cat pillow
naps on a splint-seat chair (right);
peering from the cupboard are
black-sock cats from the same period
(opposite). Next to a pitcher of
mums and bayberry, cabbage leaves
make an instant minibouquet,
tucked into a jar of baby corn.

COLLECTING
c a b i n s

Preserving a fading tradition of hand-craftmanship and a nostalgia for the romance of America's pioneer days, miniature log cabins are of special interest to Dean, who crafts cabins of his own design and also collects vintage examples. "Most of those sold today at antiques shows and auctions are from the 1920s and 1930s," he says. "Fathers used to build them for children, often as Christmas gifts, and many were made as remembrances ~ a house like the one Grandfather used to live in, for instance." Little cabins were also sold as tourist souvenirs and may bear the name of a town; "Watkins Glen, N.Y." appears on one owned by Dean. Some of the tiny axes, pitchforks, and other implements used as accessories are pieces from old jackstraws games, which were shaped like miniature tools.

The more intricate a cabin is ~ good details include chinking, individual shingles, and windows with divided lights ~ the higher its value. Although Dean has been collecting for years, he has never discovered a cabin with chinked logs, so he started making his own, using 18th-century lath for the logs and mortar for the chinking. Like the admired craftsmen of old, Dean, too, often works from memory: Many of his designs are based on historic cabins he has seen in Cades Cove, Tennessee, a pioneer community abandoned in the late 1920s when the area became part of the state's Great Smoky Mountains National Park.

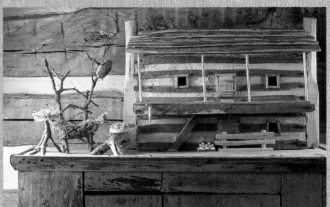

thanks

"This is a day
for appreciation ~
and for eating!"

giving

Thanksgiving at the farm is a day to pause and celebrate with family and friends, who arrive midday to feast and fraternize. The house, of course, is more than ready. White Lumina pumpkins as pale as moonglow play a large part in the holiday decorations, set atop mantels and tables along with squash, gourds, acorns, and fall leaves. Left over from Halloween, the gourds and pumpkins stay fresh until Thanksgiving, and sometimes last all winter.

The kitchen is the holiday staging area, and conversation flows from room to room as the meal is prepared. The Thanksgiving menu at Seven Gates is traditional, including mashed potatoes, sweet potatoes, green beans, corn, and brussels sprouts seasoned with the last of the fresh dill snipped from the garden. Friends bring the turkey, stuffed with sage dressing, and dessert: plump home-baked apple-cinnamon pies topped with oven-browned autumn leaves cut from pastry. After dinner, everyone drives to the mountains, where a walk in the woods yields enough berries, red sumac blooms, acorns, and black-berried greenbrier vines to fashion wreaths and other decorations that will ready their houses for Christmas.

The oak-log understructure of the house is clearly visible in the kitchen, where preparations for Thanksgiving dinner are underway. A majolica pitcher and matching mugs shaped like ears of corn serve an aromatic brew of spiced apple cider. Hung to the left of the window is a feed bag dating to 1865; the 150-year-old stepback cupboard, from the Shenandoah Valley, holds white ironstone and pewter.

165

Decorations gathered from around the house suit the autumnal theme. On a twig corner piece from West Virginia (right), baskets are displayed one to a shelf to show off individual shapes. Homespun blankets make a toasty backdrop for the holiday feast (below), while white pumpkins and candles are fresh, cool accents in the fall color scheme. The shelves hold James's collection of schoolbooks, covered in calico and homespun by young students in the 1800s.

The best decorations are often the simplest, a premise proved by this appealing pile of squash, gourds, and tiny pumpkins (above left). Dean's eye for whimsy is evident in his handcrafted turkeys; the ruffled plumage was dabbed on the scrap-tin tail with white paint (above right). Toes in the air, sunflowers dangle from a birch branch just below the dining room mantel (left).

*A dry sink draped with a linen
sheet holds the Thanksgiving
buffet, which includes green beans,
brussels sprouts, corn, bread, and
pumpkin pie nestled into a
mound of pumpkins and squash.
The centerpiece of the display
is a bouquet of bittersweet, allium,
autumn leaves, sunflowers, and
hydrangea. "I just go into the
gardens and pick whatever is left
dried on their stems," says James.*

rag dolls

Stitched with workbasket scraps and plenty of loving care, homemade rag dolls were the long-ago alternative to expensive store-bought playthings. The dollmakers' work shows amazing imagination and artistry: Coifs might be made of feathers, black fabric, or knotty lambswool, and the stuffings improvised with sawdust, straw, hair, quilt batting, or rags. Charming details often appear, such as finely stitched eyebrows or a "ring" made of gold thread like that adorning the finger of one of James and Dean's dolls.

Currently, the collection at Seven Gates comprises some 120 rag dolls dating from the late 1700s to the early 1900s. James and Dean prefer the more primitive, well-loved examples and look for dolls "as found," complete with the soil and wear left behind from years of play. Cleaning an old rag doll, in fact, decreases its value; so will washing or replacing clothes.

The face, of course, gives a doll its character. Features were typically drawn on with pencil or ink or embroidered, and the cheeks often colored a rosy red with crushed berries. When a doll got worn, a new face was sometimes stitched on over the old. The more details that distinguish a doll, the higher its value; for example, one with fingers or a profile (three-dimensional nose and ears) is considered an especially good find.

W I N

This is a time of peace and solitude at Seven Gates Farm. Classical music and a crackling woodstove create a soothing

atmosphere in Dean's workshop as he fills orders for cloches and birdhouses. James putters in the greenhouse, watching the snow fall and gently drift outside. ❧ On a cold night early in December, the two men mark the onset of the season by participating in one of the prettiest and most solemn of winter occasions, when thousands of luminarias light the battlefields of nearby Antietam. As the sky darkens, they join the slow, silent procession

of cars that winds past 23,110 candles flickering on the hillsides to commemorate each life lost in

T E R

that fierce Civil War battle. ❧ Christmas is a joyous coda to the year. Preparations start with gathering greens: boughs of holly cut from the property, bay ordered by the boxful from a California winery, and glossy lemon leaves from the florist that will fade to a beautiful muted green. ❧ Happy celebrations with family and friends wind down on New Year's Day. The morning is devoted to packing up decorations, with a pause for a brunch of black-eyed peas and sauerkraut, dishes that prophesy good fortune in the year ahead. In the next weeks, the house becomes a cosy nest, filled with warm wooly blankets and dreams of an early spring. ❧

in the

gardens

Nature's paintbrush becomes pen and ink in winter months, delineating the spare skeletal trees and bare-branched bushes that form the underpinnings of the gardens at Seven Gates. James and Dean take inspiration from these stark patterns, studying each area to see what they will add and improve when spring approaches. Although it is cold out, there are still garden chores to be done. Burlap sheaths the boxwood to protect it from the winter wind; stray leaves are raked and birdbaths periodically tipped or upended so freezing water won't collect and crack them. After a storm, the men take to the shrubs with brooms so the branches won't break with the weight of snow and ice.

James and Dean are accustomed to being outdoors, and winter is no exception. Oftentimes after lunch they will pull on coats and take a walk with the dog, or just sit outside on the Adirondack chairs to get a "light fix" that recharges them for the darker days of the season. There, they delight in the antics of the birds shuttling between the barn-shaped feeder in the side yard and the birdbath in the herb garden, which is warmed by the winter sun.

An underdressed but stoic scarecrow stands tall in the chill, keeping watch over the yard. In the background is the stone foundation of the greenhouse, which was originally intended to support an old log cabin transported in pieces from the Maryland mountains. The cabin deteriorated before James and Dean had a chance to rebuild it, so the foundation found a new use when the greenhouse went up.

Snow is the magic ingredient that casts a fairy-tale glimmer on everything, capping boxwoods, fir trees, and fence posts, burying perennials beneath an insulating blanket, brightening the air, and transforming the bare and bleak into a fleeting wonderland. Embellished with a tin stocking, a bird feeder (near right) and a martin house (far right) become winter sculptures. Bee skeps and a log-cabin birdhouse ride out the cold weather in the herb garden (below).

*Bright as cardinals, an antique
wool dress and stockings dangle from
a snow-crusted clothesline (above)
in a cheering garden vignette.
Coated with mud, a trio of twig
bee skeps found in North Carolina
take on added character (left).*

*With surrounding greenery blurred
by the snowfall, the greenhouse
stands in majestic solitude (opposite).
The welcoming wreath is studded
with garden tools and tiny flower–
pots. Come spring, espaliered
pear trees will bloom on the fence
in the foreground.*

*In keeping with the one-color
theme of the white garden
(below left), winter snow blankets
the paths and shrubs. In the
topiary garden (below right), a
pyramidal trellis frosted by
the weather awaits a flowering
clematis vine.*

in the

house

A fire roaring at the hearth, satsifying meals of soups and stews, and pleasant evenings spent perusing garden catalogues for spring plants and bulbs ~ these are the signs that the long winter season has arrived at Seven Gates Farm. The subdued color scheme of late autumn, so prevalent throughout the house in earlier weeks, is now sparked by an infusion of scarlet that instantly conveys a sense of comfort and welcome. Out of closets and chests come bright red woolen petticoats, hunting jackets, long underwear, and thick stockings collected and displayed for their warm hues. Blankets are thrown over tables, rag carpets are rolled out upstairs, and the beds are piled high with fluffy comforters.

As the days grow short, a sense of peace falls over the farmhouse. Every night at dusk, candles are lit and the kitchen fireplace re-stoked. In a Dutch oven suspended from a crane over the fire, orange peels, cinnamon, and apples simmer in water, sending an earthy fragrance into every room. This is the time of day, and the time of year, when James and Dean settle in to dream up new designs for projects in the coming months.

Tokens reminiscent of summer can temper winter's bite and hold the season at bay for the moment. Amaryllis blooming in individual pots and a garland of lemon leaves and dried roses are harbingers of cheer.

Set quietly by a fallen bird's nest, an old watering can holds a clutch of dried hydrangeas and honeysuckle (right). Dean's collection of antique cabins and mountain instruments, made of gourds and boxes, go on display in winter months (below left). James's festive trees are made by covering Styrofoam forms with spongy gray–white reindeer moss, pine cones, dried whole limes, Queen Anne's lace, and pop-corn berries (below right). Old wood balusters make handy stands.

During cold weather, the outdoors comes inside at Seven Gates. Dean made a fanciful trellis decorated with crows and propped it behind his whitewashed birdhouse (above left). A basket of popcorn berries sits on the table (above right). Warm-spirited decorations (left) include miniature twig chairs with woven rush seats, a bowl of potpourri, and a tiny pine-needle nest of acorns on a little table carved from a single piece of wood.

On chilly mornings, a good blaze
in the kitchen fireplace quickly warms
the room. As a tribute to Mother
Nature, the mantel is festooned with
a garland of bay leaves and nuts
(above); a bird's nest nestles in a
grapevine wreath studded with seed
pods above. The trellis box holds
twin "topiaries" with moss globes
and twig stems.

A nosy crow (opposite), James's
favorite bird, investigates a pair of
bird's nests in a basket above the
fireplace; socks and homespun blankets
hang to the left. The rustic hearth of
half-bricks camouflages a drab
slab of concrete.

Cosy just to look at, red woolen petticoats and homespun dresses and bonnets join a pair of high-button shoes on a peg rack in the corner bedroom (above). Stacked on the folk-art corner shelf is a collection of miniature houses, once part of the Christmas villages that circled holiday trees years ago. On the guest room wall (right), a circa-1900 wool crib quilt mirrors primitive stuffed toys taking a nap on a pillow. A red calico coverlet and a checkerboard Pennsylvania comforter, called a hap, warm the bed.

Dean whittled twig clothespins to clip old Amish mittens (left) and cotton long johns from the turn of the century (below left) to indoor clotheslines. The 1900 New Hampshire sled, hand-painted by a child, is decorated with diminutive socks and a baby's hat. Fiery wool socks and mittens trail from pegs (below right) above a miniature lake cabin, complete with screened porch, log bench, and a pair of bark canoes.

blankets

Warm and reminiscent of hearth and home, blankets hold an important place in the history of textiles, preserving a record of changing technology and tastes. The oldest blankets in James's collection, which date from the mid-19th century, are stitched from homespun, a coarse plain-weave fabric made from hand-spun yarns. The typical hand loom was rather narrow (a comfortable width to move a shuttle back and forth), so bedcoverings made at home had to be stitched from two pieces of cloth; each as wide as the loom, these were seamed in the center to make a full-size blanket. Patterns were usually simple plaids, checks, or stripes, which were easy to work in a cross weave. Blue, brown, red, and pumpkin, made with natural dyes, were popular colors.

To most collectors, the fiber of a blanket is less important than its visual impact. Because they often boast eye-catching patterns and weaves, more recently manufactured blankets made with synthetic dyes and fibers ~ including vintage examples from the 1920s, 1930s, and 1940s ~ are interesting, and are easier to find and more affordable than the earlier bedcoverings. James also collects beautifully made reproductions from the hands of contemporary craftspeople who weave traditional textiles on antique or old-style looms. Any woolen blanket should be stored in camphor or cedar mothballs when it is not being used.

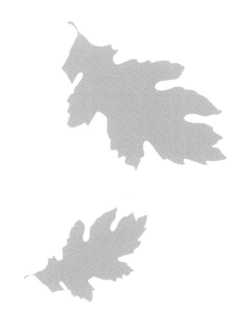

day

*Naturally decorated moss balls
pile into a green-painted rye basket
to become a festive centerpiece
for the kitchen table. James designs
the ornaments with twig stems ~
tied with raffia bows ~ to look
like miniature topiaries, and
also hangs them on Christmas trees.
Made of pottery, the pine-cone
candle holders flanking the bowl
date from the 1950s.*

Christmas is the highlight of the year at Seven Gates and a festive spirit reigns over the farm from the first of December ~ even earlier if James has his way. After months spent in their workshops and traveling to shows, James and Dean enjoy staying in Keedysville for the holidays, basking in the peace and calm of home. On Christmas Eve, they share a meal that has been a tradition in James's family for as long as he can remember: oysters dipped in beaten egg and cracker crumbs, fried, and served on potato rolls. One present is opened after supper, but the rest are saved until Christmas morning. Family arrive for Christmas dinner in the afternoon.

All visitors are greeted with the joys of the season from the moment they set foot inside the farmhouse, where something pretty rewards the senses at every turn. A white candle flickers in each window and ornaments made and collected over the years have emerged from their wrappings. The air is filled with the fragrance of paperwhite narcissus bulbs, blooming in terra-cotta dishes, china bowls, and tall metal flower buckets, as well as the fresh scent of balsam and fir from the numerous trees ~ both large and small ~ that

193

Homemade cookies and James's applesauce cake ~ an annual Christmas tradition ~ are the stars of the holiday dessert table in the kitchen (above). The tree in this room is always decorated with some kind of cookies (far right); here, angels with bay-leaf wings join holly sprigs, strings of popcorn and cranberries, and button-studded stockings filled with tiny gingerbread men. Fabric birds roost in a bagged Southern pine (near right).

James and Dean put up all through the house. Decorations conjured up with natural ingredients from yard and greenhouse appear like magical woodland visions on doors, mantels, shelves, windowsills, and tabletops, their compositions changing from year to year, and even week to week. In the living room, a mistletoe nest might be perched atop a stack of the 19th-century fabric-covered books that James collects. Red poinsettias and green topiaries pose on plant stands covered with festive scarlet tablecloths. A green wreath accented with fruit and pine cones hangs in the kitchen.

The mood outside the farmhouse is equally jubilant. Cut boxwood banks the windowsills, while garlands of western cedar ~ 75 yards in

The kitchen table often does double duty as a work space for James and Dean, who avoid holiday madness by making many of their presents and decorations from nature's bounty. Little brown bags in a wood carrier are used to organize such supplies as dried sunflower heads, acorns, and pine cones.

Beneath an 1839 sampler in the
dining room, ornaments covered with
moss and white cotton batting
transform ordinary twigs into a
magical tree that has found fragrant
housing in a dry sink filled with
potpourri (above). The miniature
wheelbarrow is loaded with
pomander balls. On the table (right),
an English cloche with leaded-
glass windows encases a bowl of pine
cones with a pot of ivy set in
the center. Hops ~ a twining vine
in the mulberry family ~ makes
a natural garland for the chandelier
and is scattered on the table.

Birch bark candles sit near a basket (below left), while candle ends in tiny flowerpots wired to an apple branch light up a natural chandelier; a piece of tin foil plugged into the drainage hole of each pot keeps wax from dripping. Spice-crusted lights made by a friend nestle in a bowl of rose hips, green apples, and dried artichokes to make an appealing centerpiece (below right).

all ~ spiral down the porch posts and swoop across the fence along South Main Street. A wood angel-head sculpture flies above the front door, which is always decorated with an oversized wreath tied with a burlap bow recycled each year. James likes to fill urns with giant Christmas orbs made of coiled grapevines or balls of chicken wire covered with boxwood and blue spruce that resemble giant topiaries.

Even the greenhouse has its own decorations. Inside the building is a little spruce tree decorated with miniature flowerpots and vintage garden tools; just outside a three-foot holly tree with balled roots is set in an urn. Its roots temporarily protected by a bed of straw, the

lighting up the season

The holidays are set aglow at Seven Gates with white lights shining in every window to symbolize the purity of the season, and bayberry and vanilla candles scenting the air. James tucks candles into mossy flowerpots, stacks them at varying levels inside a fireplace filled with pine cones, and sets fat votives directly on clay flowerpot saucers, placed wherever a corner could use atmosphere.

Holiday lights flicker outdoors, as well. To light a path to the door, James suggests setting out ice luminarias, or lanterns, as a magical way to welcome friends on a cold winter's night. These can be made by putting buckets of water outdoors: As the water freezes from the outside in, the center will still be hollow ~ after the ice is unmolded, a candle is placed in the hollow cavity left inside. Using milk cartons as molds will yield smaller ice lanterns made in the same way. Lined up on fence posts or side by side on a stone wall, these are sure to capture the spirit of Christmas.

The living room bay window is a
perfect staging area for antique
sheep, once included in scenic displays
beneath German Christmas
trees. Here, they flock among myrtle
topiaries, a pot of bushy thyme,
and a moss-filled watering can
bursting with paperwhite narcissus,
all framed by an over-arching
bend of twiggy grapevines.
The centerpiece of the arrangement
is a lush bay wreath.

201

tree will be planted in the ground after the holidays have ended.

Recently, James and Dean have also begun decorating the 15-foot pine in front of the farmhouse. A trick shared by James's father allows the men to light the venerable spruce without getting on a ladder. Strings of lights are simply caught on a nail driven sideways into the end of a long stick; as the stick is lifted here and there, the lights are snagged onto the branches. (They can be removed in the same way.) Towering over the bare herb garden, the tree now sparkles in newly lit splendor for the entire town to enjoy.

Paused mid-flight in the upstairs studio, James's heavenly angels are made from antique christening dresses and architectural fragments (opposite). Paper bags organize natural decorating ingredients (above) gathered from the gardens and yard.

Snowy accents and yet another Christmas tree ready one of three bedrooms for the holidays (above), where sweet-pea vines and Queen Anne's lace make a wreath for the peg rack. A beribboned basket keeps gift-wrapping supplies and tree decorations handy (right).

Dried artichokes on a string make an angel's jump rope (left). Slung casually over the shoulder of a ladder-back chair, a hydrangea-and-pine wreath cradles a nest of moss and hemlock cones (below left), while trees and books create an evergreen vignette on the seat. Tree decorations (below right) include angel-face ornaments, more dried artichokes embellished with star anise, and stars padded with moss and wound with satin ribbon.

christmas

trees

Each year in early December James and Dean vow to simplify the Christmas holiday when they head to the local nursery to pick out The Tree. But ideas keep percolating and every weekend presents an excuse to go out and look for more. "I can buy other things in one quick trip, but when it comes to Christmas trees, one is never enough," declares James.

Inevitably, trees of all descriptions fill the house by Christmas Eve. The largest has a place of honor in either the living room or dining room, and if it has lights, they are always white. James periodically tries a new spot and always decorates the main tree in a different way, just for the pleasure of looking at things with a fresh eye. In addition to the classic all-white light scheme, for example, he has recently tried pear-shaped lights combining red, green, and white.

A few samples of the ornaments James designs to sell every year (typically white with an angel theme) are always saved and used, and the men traditionally decorate at least one tree in gold and white, embellishing it with antique glass ornaments collected for their worn and mellow patina.

An armload of low-growing evergreens snipped from the yard makes a plump "tree"; the greens are kept fresh in a container of water tucked inside the sap bucket. Among the ornaments are star-catching angels and dried pearly everlasting. To punctuate the arrangement, a spray of pine needles and three fat pine cones are gathered casually nearby.

Chunky stars and winged angel
boots hang from a heavenly
tree festooned with dried hydrangea
(opposite, top left); bundled with
raffia, a piece of burlap covers
the balled roots (opposite, top right).
In the dining room, the largest
tree in the house (opposite, bottom left)
is arrayed with vintage white and
gold glass ornaments, wooden
stars, spice-flecked candles, and nests
of acorns (opposite, bottom right).

A cedar sapling (above left) was cut,
"planted" in an old watering can
and decorated with spun-cotton fruit
ornaments made at the turn of the
century. "Snowflakes" made of dried
Queen Anne's lace have drifted
onto the branches of two potted dwarf
Alberta spruce trees (above right).
White yarrow and sage leaves
are tucked into the dried-herb wreath.

*A Douglas fir drips with icicles
made of twisted clay dipped in pearly
paint and dusted with glitter
(below). James and Dean like to give
"living" gifts, like this little tree
perched on a plant stand (right); the
live garland of variegated ivy is
planted in the same pot and woven
through the branches as it grows.
Little white candles in tin holders
topped with pearly everlasting
are snowy accents.*

A 1920s Pine Tree quilt makes
an appropriate holiday backdrop for a
minigrove of Alberta spruces that
spring up from the trough of a dry sink
(above left). The balled roots are
wrapped in old linen tied with raffia.

A mitten tree looked lonely on
an old dresser (above right), so James
added a pair of friendly Amish
toys. Dean's handcrafted homestead
includes a Christmas log cabin
surrounded by a twig fence.

Wooden garden fairies adorn a
minitree (above left). To give pears
and pine boughs a sparkly glow,
James spritzes them with water, then
dusts on glitter. A miniature tree
(above right) is made of walnuts,
dried bittersweet leaves, and
wheat celosia flowers hot-glued to
a Styrofoam cone and set on
a towering trio of cast-iron urns
filled with nuts.

White candy canes and starry
miniature lights (opposite) can set a
tree aglow as effectively as old-
fashioned candles. James collects
vintage wrapping paper like the pine-
tree print but instead of hoarding
it, he uses it ~ then hunts down more
in the new year. Oak leaves, pine
cones, and raffia ties are simple but
charming embellishments for
papers both patterned and plain.

angel shoes

I f angels favored footwear, they would surely wear these winged boots made from scraps of wool blanket. Materials and equipment: scissors; paper for pattern; pencil; white wool; needles; gold cord; thread; tarpaper; thin scrap wood; jigsaw; black and gold metallic craft paint; glue; paint brush.

A. Cut a paper pattern in a boot shape and place on a double thickness of wool; trace with a pencil and cut. Fold down the top edge of each piece and stitch to finish. Place the pieces right sides together and stitch a ⅛-inch seam around the edge, leaving the top open. Turn the boot right side out.

B. Using a needle and gold cord, sew on the laces. Cut the ends, leaving a 6-inch excess and tie into a bow. For the sole, trace the boot bottom on the tarpaper and cut. With a jigsaw, cut a heel from the wood. Paint it black and let dry; glue to the sole, then glue the sole to the boot.

C. Fold the tarpaper in two. Cut a wing pattern leaving the fold intact. Brush both sides of each wing with gold paint. Let dry; glue the fold of the wings onto the back seam of the boot. Stitch a loop for hanging using a needle and thread.

decorated

mantels

Trimmed with narrow mantels, the old fireplaces here at Seven Gates Farm are perfect small-scale stages for James's winning displays. Like all of his decorations, these Christmas creations are usually arranged on the spur of the moment as inspiration strikes. The jumping-off point might be some interesting object recently unearthed at an antiques show, a favorite collection, or something as simple as a ribbon garland. Sometimes James gathers all-of-a-kind items ~ candlesticks, bowls, various things that share the same color ~ then goes to work, trimming here and there, adding and subtracting, until the mantel has the flair and balance he is after.

James has found most displays tend to need more, not less, and almost always benefit from layering. "It's like getting dressed, then adding the right accessory to make what you are wearing come alive," he says. A design might change midway as a mantel display evolves, and even then the results are rarely final. A bag of bright green apples, or something new from workshop, greenhouse, or studio can start the process all over again.

To show off Amish mittens, James slipped them over sand-filled bottles and added merry bracelets of holly; the swagged cranberries are draped between oversized candles. Mounted above, a Victorian barge-board with whimsical cutouts, from the roof peak of an 1880s Virginia house, becomes a dramatic sculpture. The fireside bowl is heaped with holly and pineapples; James dries these by sticking the fruits with cloves and hanging them in a wire basket for six weeks.

White wool stockings are hung
by the chimney with care, filled with
bay leaves, evergreen sprigs, and
ornaments made from a mixture of
powdered cinnamon and applesauce (right). A rusty herald angel
(below left) flies in a frame wound
with popcorn berries and crow's
foot, while German statice and lemon
leaves make a lush garland. Cranberry
vinegars and other gifts from friends
are often used in mantel displays;
pretty bottles join herb candles,
and a pepperberry wreath tied with
a ticking bow (below right).

Some of Dean's handmade cabins are just the right size for mantels. A board-and-batten version and a forest of miniature timbers (above) congregate below a 1914 hand-drawn map of the United States. A ring-sized wreath and tiny swag of pine personalize a plaster-and-lath cabin (left), with wings sheathed in beaded siding.

A glorious tableau includes
children's garden tools wired to a
moss-covered frame, a fanlight
borrowed from the greenhouse, and
a swag of acorns drilled and
strung on wire, then overlaid with
a garland of lemon leaves and
freeze-dried roses.

A NOTE FROM
james and dean

For making this book possible, we would like to thank Rachel Newman, Niña Williams, Keith Scott Morton, Anne Gridley Graves, Ann Bramson, Ella Stewart, Rachel Carley, Wendy Frost, Mary Sears, and Pat Tan.

We salute Patty Faulkner, Kathy McDonough, Jeannie Trammell, and Edie Fladung for all those antique-hunting trips; Doug Cramer for teaching us how to grow topiaries; Kathy Hoffman for sharing old photographs of Seven Gates Farm; and Marilyn Kowaleski for providing information on collecting blankets.

Many artists have graced our home with their work: Joyce Bingham (hooked carrots and rooster); Ned and Gwen Foltz (redware eggs and pottery); Glory Nicholas (garlands); Steve and Mary Petlitz (tin birds and pumpkins); Jennifer and Norma Schneeman (fabric birds and flowerpot garden pillows); Nancy Settel (herb candles); Carolyn Swain (garden fairies); Nancy Thomas (garden sign and cedar pumpkins); Mary Worley (woven blankets, pillowcases, and table runners).

And to all the wonderful friends we have met, and to those who have called or written to us asking that we do a book:

This one's for you.

index